You Know You're Really In Love When...

by Margaret Howard

**Pictures by
Jerry Zimmerman**

A Bananas Book From Scholastic Paperbacks
New York Toronto London Auckland Sydney Tokyo

ISBN 0-590-31786-5

Copyright © 1980 by Scholastic Magazines, Inc. All rights reserved. Published by Scholastic Book Services, a division of Scholastic Magazines, Inc.

12 11 10 9 8 7 6 5 4 3 2 1   11   0 1 2 3 4 5/8

Printed in the U.S.A   09

Introduction

Sure you spent six days sorting and polishing his fish hook collection. And you didn't even complain that some of them had definite worm parts still attached!

Okay, so you dream about her all the time — even during the final period of the championship hockey game — and you're the goalie!

But are you really in love???

It's not always easy to tell. What may seem like love one day could turn out to be infatuation (or just indigestion) the next! Luckily, the friendly folks at BANANAS have prepared this handy guide book for you. Here in glorious color are all the tell-tale signs — the dead give-aways and the subtle hints — that will tell you if this time, it's really, really love!

You know you're really in love when . . .

You're supposed to memorize the Gettysburg Address, but you spend a whole study period writing his name over and over again, using different colored pens.

Two years ago you got a diary for a present and have never used it. Now you write in it every day and make sure it's locked and hidden away when you're done.

You know you're really in love when . . .

Instead of playing your Meat Loaf album with friends, you listen to Frank Sinatra records by yourself.

You know you're really in love when . . .

You think his hands are beautiful, even though his nickname is Stubby.

You know you're really in love when . . .

She's an ice skater, and you take the time to learn the difference between a flying camel and a double walley.

You know you're really in love when . . .

You think it's clever and adorable of her to have eyebrows.

Usually you call your brother "House Ape," but when she's around you call him "Old Buddy."

You know you're really in love when . . .

You're happy to ride 300 miles on a bus on a rainy weekend to visit her.

You know you're really in love when . . .

You think his name — John — is the most special and beautiful name in the whole world.

You know you're really in love when . . .

You leave cute notes in her locker, written in French — correctly.

You know you're really in love when . . .

For no reason in particular, you decide to clean the inside of the family car and throw out a year's worth of Big Mac boxes, soda cans, candy wrappers, and old sneakers.

She's a vegetarian, so you ask your mother to make you a big plate of mashed yeast and sea-weed for dinner.

You know yo... ...love when ...

Your older sister offers to fix your hair, and you let her.

You know you're really in love when . . .

You stand all afternoon in the cold rain to watch his soccer team lose 12-0.

You know you're really in love when . . .

You wash your hair every day, even if it doesn't need it.

You use after-shave lotion, even though you don't shave.

You have regularly been consuming enough food to supply a Marine platoon, but now all you want is crackers and clear soup.

You pass up a chance to go to a rock concert because you'd rather help him mow the lawn.

You pay attention to the situation in Tanzania so you'll have something to talk about with her parents.

The poetry you have to read in English class begins to make sense to you.

You know you're really in love when . . .

You keep a little spray bottle of apple blossom cologne in your purse, and use it all up in a week.

You actually enjoy watching home movies of the trip her family took to Crystal Caverns when she was three years old.

You decorate your car with one of her scarves.

Your wallet contains a picture of him at his kindergarten graduation.

You know you're really in love when . . .

You think you will die if he doesn't call you.

You Know You're In Love When You Hear Yourself Saying . . .

"I love your nose. That little bump makes it so distinguished."

"You don't really have a lot of pimples."

"Isn't it fun to clean out the garage together?"

"Fang didn't really bite me — it's just a little nip. It will heal in no time."

"Sure I'll meet you before school. Seven-thirty isn't too early."

"Let's memorize geometry theorems together."

"I don't mind moving your aunt's sofa."

You Know You're In Love When You Hear Yourself Saying . . .

"Your room isn't really messy — it looks comfortable and lived-in."

"Those braces on your teeth are hardly noticeable."

"Maybe we can be lab partners. You're so good at dissecting frogs."

"You're not stupid! Anyone can get locked in a bathroom."

"It's not so bad to flunk typing — eight words a minute is pretty good, I think."

"Your little sister is cute."

"I like the way your hair sticks out."

You Know You're In Love When You Hear Yourself Saying . . .

"We don't need a car. We can walk to the show. It's only a few miles."

"Watching football practice is really interesting."

"This cake is delicious. Being flat just gives it more flavor."

"I don't mind waiting in the cafeteria line with you."

"It was a drag going skiing without you."

"No — you didn't hurt my foot. This music is just hard to dance to."

"Has it been three hours already? Time just flies when I listen to you practice the drums."

Danger Signs

Even the most thrilling romance is bound to cool off after a while. Nobody can be ecstatic all the time. But how can you tell the difference between cooling off and a definite deep freeze? How do you know when it's the beginning of The End? If you've been hearing phrases like these in the following situations, we'd say there may be trouble ahead!

On the telephone: "She's here but she told me to tell you she's not at home."
or
"Allan Schmidlapp? There's no one here by that name."

At the movies: "I can't see from here. I'm moving to that single seat, up front. See you later."

At an amusement park: "The Tunnel of Love makes me seasick. You go through and I'll meet you at the car in two hours."

After school: "I promised Miss Ratchet I'd help her organize hockey sticks. It may take quite a while. Why don't you leave without me?"

or

"I volunteered to do a special report for my social studies class on jute factories in the Yangtze River basin. I'll be spending all week in the library."

On a double date: "I get car sick if I sit in the back seat. I'll sit up in front with Todd and Katie. Okay?"

At a football game: "I just saw a girl I know from camp across the field. I've got to say hello. I'll be back after half-time."

At a dance: "My hair's a mess. I've got to go fix it." (Repeated every 20 minutes.)

At the beach: "You're getting sand all over me. Could you move over?"

Uh, oh! Maybe there really is trouble ahead! Is it curtains, fini, the last waltz, the end, split city? Quick, turn this book over and find out if it's really time to (sob) break up!

Hey, things are beginning to warm up around here! Maybe it isn't time to say good-bye after all. Quick turn this book over and find out if you've been smitten, pierced by Cupid's arrow, entranced, enraptured — if this time you're really in love!

Songs (to sing, hum, or play a lot)

Romantic	NOT Romantic
Misty	Satisfaction
Ooh, Baby, Baby	Do Ya Think I'm Sexy
Just the Way You Are	Boogie Oogie Oogie
I Honestly Love You	Great Balls of Fire
Three Times a Lady	Disco Duck
The Way We Were	Stars and Stripes Forever

Activities

Romantic	NOT Romantic
Polo	Bowling
Walking	Jogging
Canoeing	Water skiing
Tennis	Dodge ball
Collecting stamps	Collecting tin cans
Carousels	Roller coasters
Roller skating	Skateboarding

Clothes (Girls)

Romantic	NOT Romantic
A long, filmy scarf	Plastic rain hat
Long skirt	Baggies
Gloves	Mittens
Lace	Elastic
Fur muff	Knapsack
Ballet slippers	Rubber boots

Clothes (Boys)

Romantic	NOT Romantic
Old tweed jacket	Leisure suit
A leather jacket	Straw hat with beer cans on it
Loafers without socks	Black shoes with white socks
An old wool sweater	Banlon sport shirt
Trench coat	Slicker

Food

Romantic
Strawberries
Lobster
Mushrooms
Chocolate mousse
Artichokes
Almonds
Crusty French bread
Lemonade
Snow peas
Trout

NOT Romantic
Prunes
Knockwurst
Brussels sprouts
Scooter pies
Cottage cheese
Jello
Oatmeal
Yoo-Hoo
Parsnips
Scrod

Music-Makers, Movies, and Books

Romantic
The Beatles
Olivia Newton-John
Love Story
Gone with the Wind
Star Wars
King Kong
Wuthering Heights

The Prophet

NOT Romantic
Kiss
Bette Midler
Orca, the Killer Whale
Benji
Star Trek
Godzilla
How To Flatten
  Your Stomach
Heloise's Helpful
  Household Hints

Gifts

Romantic
Perfume
Book of poetry

Flowers
Fountain pen
Anything made of silk

Diary

Handmade sweater

NOT Romantic
Mouthwash
The Wonderful World
  of Iguanas
A calculator
Bic pen
Anything made of
  polyester
Calendar from Al's
  Auto Body &
  Wrecking Service
Handmade socks

Everything You Need To Know About Romance

By now you should know if you're really in love or if it's time to break up. But what about those borderline cases? Some relationships can be warmed up before they cool to the freezing point. All you have to do is put a little more romance in your romance.

But wait a minute. It isn't as easy as running out and buying candy and flowers. That won't help a bit if the flowers are ragweed and the candy is breath mints! You've got to know what's romantic and what's not. Luckily, BANANAS has compiled this handy chart for you to consult. The chart may not show you the way to that special someone's heart — but it should show the way to some hearty laughs!

It's Time To Break Up When You Hear Yourself Saying . . .

"Your hair looks weird. What did you do to it, anyway?"

"Wow! My uncle just invited me to visit him in Gopher Junction for two months! It should be really exciting!"

"You need a shampoo."

"Sorry, I have to stay home and organize my sock drawer."

"Don't bother waiting for me."

"Slow dancing gets really boring after a while."

"I can't talk now — one of my guppies is sick."

It's Time To Break Up
When You
Hear Yourself Saying . . .

"You don't mind if my cousin comes along, do you?"

"Can't you get someone else to go with you on your babysitting job? I have a hang nail."

"Have you tried using dental floss?"

"Keep your eyes on the road and turn up the radio."

"I think I'll go home. There's nothing good on TV."

"I'd like to get in early tonight, for a change."

"Ralph, Bill, Stanley, and Chuck are coming with us. They're so much fun!"

It's Time To Break Up When You Hear Yourself Saying . . .

"Is that the dress you're so excited about?"

"Maybe I'll take up sky diving."

"Maybe it would help if you cut out desserts and bread."

"This drive is so boring. Wake me up when we get there."

"My house is just down the block. You can leave me right here at the corner."

"Why didn't you tell me it was your birthday?"

"There just wasn't enough room in my wallet for your picture. I have to carry my Junior Space Cadet card, don't I?"

You know it's time to break up when . . .

You find yourself doodling someone else's initials on your notebook.

You imagine yourself a year from now, and she's not in the picture.

It's ten minutes before you're supposed to meet her and you're still in the backyard trying to teach Spot to roll over.

You envy your little sister because she's in fourth grade and too young for boys.

Your best friend says he doesn't want to double date with you because you and your girlfriend argue too much.

You avoid the quiet, little, out-of-the-way place you used to like, and now hang out where there'll be at least 20 people you know.

You know it's time to break up when . . .

You're looking forward to your junior class trip to the state capital, even though she's a sophomore.

You're secretly relieved when your parents insist that you stay at home and write a book report on <u>Ivanhoe</u>.

You return the earrings he gave you, exchange them for another pair, and he never notices the difference.

You know it's time to break up when . . .

You're glad it's Monday.

You know it's time to break up when . . .

You'd rather eat in the biology lab among the preserved brains than meet him for a cozy lunch at "your table" in the cafeteria.

You have a choice between a Valentine's Day dance and a family get-together with all your aunts and uncles, and you choose the latter.

You no longer vacuum the cat hair off the sofa before he comes over.

You know it's time to break up when . . .

You prefer going someplace with a deafening rock band so you won't have to make much conversation.

You know it's time to break up when . . .

Instead of waiting around for him to call, you go out and tell your sister to take the message.

You meet someone new who asks if you've got a boyfriend, and you say no.

He suggests a romantic walk in the gentle spring rain, but you decide you don't want to get your umbrella wet.

You know it's time to break up when . . .

You order a chili dog with extra onions.

You know it's time to break up

You keep her waiting while you and a friend play a hot game of Old Maid.

You know it's time to break up when . . .

You get tired of hearing "Our Song" and pretending that it's special.

You know it's time to break up when . . .

You read two chapters of Silas Marner while talking to her on the phone.

You know it's time to break up when . . .

Your mother asks you to take your kid brother along on a date — and you don't mind.

Your father yells at you to get off the phone, and you don't argue.

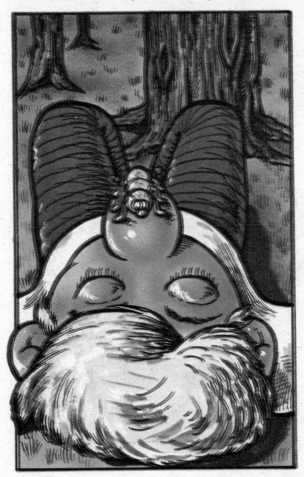

You go on a picnic and fall asleep.

You know it's time to break up when . . .

You'd rather stay home and shampoo your dog than go to a disco with your boyfriend.

Introduction

Let's face it — no matter what you may think at the time, being in love doesn't last forever. Eventually the bloom fades from the rose, the music stops, the party's over, the thrill is gone . . . and it's time to think about breaking up.

But how can you tell the difference between a romance that's just settling down and getting comfortable and one that is definitely dead and not worth reviving? When do you know it's time to break up?

This BANANAS guide will give you the answers to these puzzling questions — so that maybe breaking up won't be so hard to do.

BANANAS Books are brought to you by BANANAS, today's most insane magazine for teenagers.
Editorial Director/BANANAS Books: Jane Stine.
Design Director: Bob Feldgus.
Production Manager: Judith Gorman.

You Know It's Time To Break Up When...

by Margaret Howard

**Pictures by
Jerry Zimmerman**

A Bananas Book From Scholastic Paperbacks
New York Toronto London Auckland Sydney Tokyo